BOLLINGTON
The Cheshire Cat That Lost Its Grin

Each morning at precisely nine o'clock Bollington would open his eyes, yawn, and check the weather outdoors.

If it was sunny, he would grin. If it was raining, he would grin. If the wind was blowing so strongly that leaves were torn from the branches of trees ... have you guessed? He would grin.

Bollington brushed his teeth to keep them shiny white, combed his fur to keep it neat and free of knots and polished his claws to keep them clean and sharp. Bollington was a Cheshire Cat and Cheshire cats are famous for their grin.

After he had sipped a saucer of milk and eaten a bowl of cereal, he brushed his teeth again and practiced saying *'meow'* with a Cheshire accent. The final task for Bollington was to check in the mirror that his grin was still in place before he went out for his morning stroll in the garden. Cheshire cats are famous for their grin, as we've already said.

Bollington screeched! "Me-ooow!"

The Cheshire cat he saw in the mirror did *not* have a grin on its face!

Bollington closed his eyes and then opened them again.

The cat staring back at him in the mirror *still* had no grin on its face, let alone a smile.

A proper Cheshire cat *always* wore a grin.

Where had it gone? He didn't think Richard Robin would have borrowed it during the night because it would be too wide to fit in his beak. He didn't think Percy Pigeon would have flown away with it because he never got out of bed until late in the morning to deliver the post. He did not think Ollie Owl had taken it either because he was too busy at night reading books and being wise.

So ...where was his grin?

Bollington decided to ask his friends in The Undermead Woods if any of them had seen his grin on their journeys in and around the trees. The first friend he found was

Happy Hedgehog.

"You're not looking at all cheerful this morning," Happy said.

Bollington sighed.

"I'm not *feeling* at all cheerful," he replied.

"I've lost my grin."

"Have you looked in the red cherry bush?"

"Do you think it might be there?" Bollington asked.

"Well, the cherries always look cheerful. They certainly have *something* to smile about," Happy said.

"Maybe your grin is hiding behind the cherries. Why not take a look?"

"That's a good idea. Thank you, Happy." Bollington walked towards the bush and looked carefully behind the red cherries, but his grin was not hiding in the red cherry bush.

Bollington spotted Squeaky Squirrel

scrambling down a tree trunk.

"Hello, Squeaky! I've lost my grin. Have you seen it hiding in the branches of the trees?"

"No, but there's a weeping willow beside the brook," Squeaky replied.

"A weeping willow tree doesn't sound like a place where a grin would hide," Bollington said in a sad voice.

"Unless the grin wanted to stop the willow weeping and cheer it up," Squeaky said.

"I suppose you could be right," Bollington

agreed. "Thank you. I'll go and look."

But the grin was not there either.

Bollington walked into a field of beautiful daffodils and new-born lambs.

"Are you looking for someone?" Bollington looked over his shoulder at his tail.

"Did you say something to me?" he asked

his tail.

"Don't be silly! It was *me*, Tommy Tortoise."

"Oh, hello, Tommy! What are you doing out in the open? Surely the sun is in your eyes?"

"Nonsense! I always wear a sunhat on days like this."

"That's sensible," Bollington said.

"You look as though you've lost something," Tommy said.

"I have, indeed! I've lost my grin and a Cheshire cat without its grin is like the centre of a giant hula hoop."

"How so?" Tommy Tortoise asked.

"There's a big hole in the middle where its grin should be!" "Oh, dear. I hope you find it. Sorry, but I must dash. I'm chasing Sammy Snail."

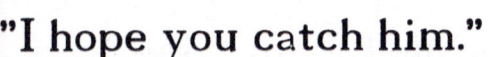

"I hope you catch him."

"I usually do. He doesn't train as hard as

me."

Bollington stopped to rest.

"Perhaps I put my grin in a secret hiding place but can't remember where the secret hiding place is," he said out loud.

"Perhaps you did!" Bollington leapt into the air with fright.

"My apologies. It was not my intention to startle you," said a familiar voice.

"Ollie Owl! You caught me by surprise," Bollington said. "Maybe you can use your wisdom to solve my problem."

"My wisdom can *always* solve a problem," Ollie replied solemnly.

"I've lost my grin," Bollington explained, "and a Cheshire cat without a grin is simply ... a cat!"

"A cat," Ollie Owl remarked in a very wise voice, "**is** known as a *feline.*"

"Is that so?" Bollington asked. "It is. And when we find your grin, and the grin is

back on your face, you will be *feline fine! Hoot! Hoot!"*

"Very funny, Ollie. Now, do you have a wise plan that will help me find it?"

"Of course! After all, I helped a glow worm that had lost its glow."

"Really? What did you do?"

"I suggested he ate *a light meal. Hoot! Hoot!"*

"Very funny. Ho! Ho! Ho! Now, do you have

a wise plan, or should I look for another wise owl?"

"You will not find a wiser owl the whole wide world."

"I do not want to find a wiser owl. I simply want to find my grin!"

"Follow me," Ollie Owl said to Bollington. "I have a wise idea."

Bollington looked worried. "Oh, dear," he said. "I can't follow you."

"Why is that?" Ollie Owl asked.

"You have wings to fly and I only have my purr and a tail to wag."

"I do not expect a Cheshire Cat to fly," Ollie said in a patient voice. "We shall walk, of course, so you will have no problem following me."

"Are we going to look for a saucer of milk?"

"No. We are going to look for a Squeaky Squirrel!"

***

Squeaky Squirrel was busy brushing up

leaves that had fallen from an old oak tree into a tidy pile. He looked up when he spotted Ollie Owl and Squeaky Squirrel.

"Hello, Ollie. Hello, Bollington. Have you come to bring me some nuts that I can hide beneath these leaves ready for winter?"

"That is not the purpose of our visit today," Ollie replied. "

Have you come to brush my bushy tail?" Squeaky Squirrel asked politely.

"Certainly not! I have no time for such small

matters. I am the wisest owl in the whole wide world, and I have lots of books to read and write."

Squeaky Squirrel looked disappointed. "So, how can I help you today?" he asked politely. Ollie Owl opened his large, round eyes very wide.

"*Aha*," he said as something bright and cheerful caught his eye.

"Have you been polishing those nuts that you are trying to hide beneath a pile of leaves with beeswax?" he asked.

"Certainly not!" Squeaky Squirrel replied. "*The Undermead Fruit and Nut Shop* had sold out of it. I'm simply preparing my winter drey and I don't want anyone to find my nuts and steal them."

Bollington looked at Ollie Owl.

"What is *a winter drey?*" he asked.

"That, my friend," Ollie replied with a *very* wise look on his face, "is the name given to the winter home of a squirrel."

"You are *so* wise," Bollington sighed. "But do you have a wise plan to help me find my grin?" he asked.

"Of course," Ollie replied and he strutted towards the pile of leaves.

"Hey!" squeaked Squeaky Squirrel. "Don't go stealing my nuts." My dear friend," Ollie said with a hugh sigh,

"I have no intention of stealing your nuts *this* is what I intend to take."

Both Squeaky Squirrel and Bollington watched as Ollie Owl strutted forward and poked his beak into the pile of leaves that was covering the nuts Squeaky had been trying to hide.

They heard Ollie hoot, '*Gotcha*' and a few

seconds later his beak poked through the leaves and reappeared holding something bright and cheerful in its grip. Something that looked *very* cheerful.

It was Bollington's *grin!*

"ME...OOOW!" Bollington said loudly.

"Well, I never!" exclaimed Squeaky Squirrel. "It must have crept into the leaves while I wasn't looking."

"*A-hem*," Ollie Owl said. "My *very* wise plan was *very* successful, don't you think?"

"Thank you *so* much, Ollie! What *was* your wise plan?"

Before Ollie could reply, Percy Pigeon dived down from the sky and landed on Ollie's head.

"I *almost* managed a mid-air somersault," he

said and then added, "but I *do* have a brand-new poem for you both."

Ollie Owl sighed. "Very well, Let's hear it then."

'Ollie had a plan

To find a Cheshire grin,

But I saw it *creep* away

And *hide* behind a bin.

Then to the woods it *scuds*

To find a place to hide

And finds a warm and cosy home

In Squeaky Squirrel's nuts.'

Ollie Owl puffed out his chest.

'Thank you, Percy. I couldn't have put it better myself."

And then, a moment or two later, to

everyone's delight, Bollington cried "*Ouch!*" as the grin leapt up from the pile of leaves and settled on his face. his face.

Bollington now grinned a grin that could only be found on the face of a Cheshire Cat!

"I thought you had run away and that I might never see you again," Bollington said.

The grin tried to say, "I know where I belong," but it couldn't talk so it simply curled up on Bollington's face and fell fast asleep with a grin on its face.

"Me-ooow!" "Me-ooow!"

"Me-ooow!"

WHISKERS and WINGS

(Tales of Countryside Companions)

~~~

BLACKBERRY PIE

Happy Hedgehog was not feeling very happy.

He had overslept but had arranged to meet his daughter at a quarter to breakfast time. His stomach was rumbling and he knew he would need to hurry.

Happy was pleased with his new winter coat and hat and waterproof walking shoes for splashing through the puddles that had appeared everywhere after the heavy rain of the previous night.

Happy Hedgehog was not happy. He had tried to brush his bristles before setting out to meet his daughter but something was getting in the way. He tugged on his comb. He tugged harder. He tugged even harder and the comb came free.

"Hello," said Andy Ant hopping down from the comb and landing beside him.

"Hope you didn't mind but I needed somewhere dry to sleep last night."

"Well, I do mind. I'm not a home for homeless ants," Happy said.

Happy Hedgehog had almost reached his daughter's house.

"Good morning," said Sammy Snail who happened to be passing at the time.

"I just love this wet weather," he said. "Give

me a puddle to splash in and I'm a very contented little snail. Are you off to visit Henrietta?" he enquired.

"Yes. My daughter's expecting me and I'm already late," Happy replied. "So, goodbye, Andy. We must meet up soon when I have more time" and he sped away at full speed.

"I'm glad I have a shell over my head," Sammy Snail thought. "Those prickles of his could scratch my face and damage my complexion" and he slid away to look for another friend to talk to.

*

Henrietta Hedgehog was waiting at the door as her father arrived.

"Daddy" she cried even before he had removed his hat. "Roland Rabbit has stolen the blackberries I had ready for our breakfast."

"Are you sure?" he asked. Roland Rabbit was usually blamed when food went missing ... even if he was on holiday at the time!

"Well, we'd better go across the field and

pay him a visit," said Happy Hedgehog.

*

Henrietta Hedgehog and her father made their way slowly across the muddy field. Happy was delighted with his waterproof walking shoes but his daughter was grumbling.

"I washed my spines only last night and now look at them!" she complained. "I hope you will point that out to Roland Rabbit. It's his fault."

Her father turned and gave her a very slightly angry look.

"Nothing is Roland's fault. Not yet, anyway." It rarely was, he thought.

*

They reached Roland's cosy house deep below the roots of an old oak tree and knocked on the door. "Coming!" said a cheerful voice and one bunny-hop moment later Roland Rabbit was welcoming them with a huge smile.

"Come in and sit down," he said, "but watch your heads ... the ceiling is quite low."

Happy Hedgehog was just a moment too late and felt his new hat being crushed on the ceiling before it fell to the floor.

"I'm having the builders in next week to raise the ceiling above ear height," Roland remarked as he picked up Happy's hat from the floor.

There were a few more pleasantries and then Roland said,

"Can I offer you some refreshments? I have a jug of delicious blackberry juice that I made only this morning."

"Oh!" exclaimed Henrietta Rabbit. "What a coincidence! I was going to make some this morning, too, until ... somebody ... stole ... my ...blackberries."

"Um ..." Happy Hedgehog began to say, "We were, um, just wondering, um, if, *um*, you might have seen, anyone with, *um*, blackberries while you were out this morning?"

"Goodness me, yes," replied Roland Rabbit. "It was really quite amusing. That rascally Curly Cat was wearing a blackberry necklace when we bumped into each other by the tractor. He said he was going to a fancy-dress party."

There was a moment's pause.

"I see," Henrietta Hedgehog said, "and where exactly did you get your blackberries from?"

"Why, by the hedge behind the old sheds," Roland Rabbit replied. "Just about where I saw young George gathering blackberries before you arrived."

George was the young boy who lived at The Big House. They all looked out of the door and saw George rubbing a blackberry over his nose.

There was a moment's pause. A rather long moment's pause before Happy Hedgehog said,

"Um, yes, well I think we might collect a few as we happen to be in the neighbourhood. Sorry we can't stay. Just called to see that you were all right after the storm last night."

*

Henrietta Hedgehog and her father arrived back home with their pockets full of blackberries.

"Well," said Happy Hedgehog as they emptied the blackberries from their pockets and placed them on the kitchen table,

"Roland Rabbit had no need to take other people's blackberries."

"No," said Henrietta. "I feel really guilty for ... for almost accusing him of ... theft."

"Well, you didn't. That's the important thing," her father said.

"Why don't you bake him one of your famous blackberry pies? I'll collect it this evening and take it to him."

"What a splendid idea!" exclaimed Henrietta. "Would you mind checking inside the oven for me? I think I may have left some plates in it last night. The rain was so heavy I was worried about everything being washed away."

"That's because the hinges on your front doors are loose! They need adjusting."

"Another job for me tonight!" he sighed.

Happy Hedgehog crossed the floor to the oven.

He opened the oven door.

"Henrietta!" he exclaimed. "Come here, will

you, please."

Henrietta crossed the floor to join her father.

He pointed. She looked.

Resting on the middle shelf in the oven was a bowl.

In the bowl *there were blackberries*.

"Well ..." Henrietta began to say,

"I remember now ... I put them in the oven so that Roland Rabbit wouldn't find them."

Her father stiffened his bristles and said,

"You should not have suspected that Roland Rabbit would steal them. That was wrong."

"I know that now," said Henrietta almost in tears ... and then a large smile appeared on her face.

"I will bake a blackberry pie for Roland Rabbit and take it to his house while it is still warm."

"What a splendid idea" her father exclaimed.

That evening ... Roland Rabbit sat on a little

chair at a little table and tucked into the most delicious blackberry pie he had ever tasted. Actually, it was the first blackberry pie he had ever tasted as he did not know how to bake and, anyway, he didn't have an oven. But he was content.

That evening ... Henrietta Hedgehog said *'good night'* to Roland Rabbit and made her way back home with a big smile on her face. She felt very happy.

*

That evening ... Happy Hedgehog kissed his

daughter goodnight and set off back across the field to his home. He was happy, too, but then, of course, he was always Happy!

A short story for Junior and Adult readers

THE DOUGHNUT MAN

"Here he comes," said Daisy, nudging the girl beside her.

"Who?" asked the girl.

"The **doughnut** man," Daisy replied.

"Oh," said the girl in a disinterested tone.

"Everyday," Daisy continued, "Everyday he comes here, round about eleven and buys a doughnut. Missed him one day, though - it was a Thursday, I think. I said to him, "didn't see you yesterday." "No," he replied, "had a bad stomach."

Turning to her customer, Daisy asked, "What will it be today, Harry? The usual?"

Harry hated her using his name like that - the over-familiarity - but she had asked him once and he had stupidly told her.

"Yes, please, dear."

She poured him a cup of percolated coffee, added cream, selected the largest of the remaining doughnuts and put it on a plate.

"One pound," demanded the other girl from behind the till.

Harry wiped the sugar off his hands with the white serviette and shuffled back his chair. Still shuffling, he made his way out of the coffee parlour towards the furniture department and the way out. As he passed the cake counter Daisy shouted over to him,

"Have a nice day!" He detested that expression.

"Thank you," he mumbled, turning towards her.

"Anything special today?" asked Daisy before he had time to retreat.

"Oh, - oh, yes, of course," replied Harry. "Having tea with some young friends. It'll be jolly fun. Lots to do. Very exciting." After a moment's reflection, he added, "never lonely."

*

Daisy was not bright but then again, she wasn't stupid. Harry's last words revolved in her mind for the rest of the day.

"Never lonely," he had said. She pondered. Why was it that she so often felt lonely, she with all her friends and discos and seven hundred pounds saved towards a second-hand car? She didn't think a cup of coffee and a doughnut could help make life more exciting even if it contented old Harry. Must be those young friends of his - grandchildren, no doubt, and his grown-up family. She decided it was probably a good thing to have young people around you when you grew old and that's what she would do when her time came.

Mind, she would have to get married and have

children in between and none of her numerous boyfriends seemed likely to suggest marriage although they never seemed short of **other** suggestions!

Still, a new car - a second-hand car - would change all that.

Independence. That's what she needed. Independence. Get out and about. On her own. In-de-pen-dence.

*

If the Coffee Parlour thought it had an exclusive claim on Harry's business, it was wrong. They shouldn't assume that because he went there every morning, barring occasional stomach-ache, that he didn't go somewhere else in the afternoon. He went to Woolworth's at around two o'clock for afternoon tea and a doughnut and to Pringles Coffee Shop for a glass of orange juice at about four o'clock. Not forgetting another doughnut, of course. These were very busy places and his regular comings and goings were barely noticed. If they were, they were not commented upon and, anyway, the staff changed with such regularity that they would never have had the opportunity to discover that he was a "regular".

*

One Monday morning, the other girl yawned and asked Daisy, "What's the time?"

"Eleven o'clock," replied Daisy, not even glancing at her watch.

"That's clever. How d'you know that?" The other girl looked at her with a mixture of curiosity and admiration.

"'Cos here comes the doughnut man," smiled Daisy.

"Did you have a pleasant weekend, Harry?" she enquired.

He wished she wasn't so familiar. Shouldn't she really address him as "Sir" or, more appropriately, "Mr. Coker"?

He likes me calling him Harry, thought Daisy.

"Yes, thank you," he said stiffly. Then more brightly, "I had tea with the youngsters. I played "Teddy Bears Picnic" on my gramophone and then we listened to the radio."

"No telly, then?" interjected the other girl.

"The picture box?" Harry enquired quizzically.

"Oh, no, we never get lonely with the radio. If we kept *seeing* pictures with people in, well, that would make us very lonely, wouldn't it? **Seeing** them but not really **being** with them. **Hearing** them, without seeing their faces, sort of makes them not exist. Much better."

*

Daisy bought her second-hand car. It wasn't much to look at but then she hadn't paid much. As she sat behind the steering wheel, she said to herself "In-de-pen-dence". Strangely, though, she didn't feel independent. She felt lonely. Sitting behind the wheel, with nowhere in particular to go and nobody in particular she wanted to see, made her feel, well, lonely. Why she should suddenly think of Harry she didn't know but she did. She envied him a little. Coffee and doughnuts, young folk and the radio. It all sounded so cosy. It all sounded so **silly,** thought Daisy angrily, and slammed the car into gear and drove away.

*

The other girl shrieked loudly as Harry shuffled to the counter.

Daisy rushed from the back room, caught sight

of Avis wavering between crying or fainting and demanded "Whatever is it?"

The other girl stabbed a finger in the direction of Harry.

"It's wrapped in brown paper! *It's a baby* - and it's wrapped in brown paper!"

Under Harry's arm was a brown paper parcel and poking out from what, presumably, was the top, there was a head of hair.

"What **have** you got there, Harry?" asked Daisy, ignoring the feeble figure beside her.

"It's a new addition to the family," muttered Harry, resenting the familiar use of his name and his involuntary reply.

"Why, it's only a doll," laughed the other girl.

"It may be only a doll to you, my girl, but it means rather more than that to some other folk," choked Harry crossly as he grabbed, and spilt, his coffee into the saucer on which he'd balanced a doughnut.

When he was out of earshot and seated at a table, Daisy turned to the other girl and scalded,

"You should know better than to laugh like that, Avis. Don't you know *anything*? 'Course he's lonely, really, and lonely people like giving presents. It makes them feel wanted. His granddaughter will be so ***thrilled***'.

But the other girl had forgotten Daisy's words long before Harry had tottered out of the Coffee Parlour.

The other girl was on her day-off the next morning when Harry dropped in for his coffee and doughnut. Daisy wondered if she should apologise for Avis' behaviour and whether she could dare ask him what was in today's parcel.

Before she could make a decision, Harry volunteered, "I've got some pretty little items of clothing here." He patted a small package.

"And who would **they** be for?" Daisy asked conversationally but not a degree of curiosity.

"For my special little baby," replied Harry.

"Oh, that's nice," said Daisy, not knowing quite what else to say. He must dote on his grandchildren.

"Yes," continued Harry, "it's my birthday soon.

We're going to have just a teeny-weeny celebration and I do want all my little friends to look pretty."

"They must be looking forward to it?" ventured Daisy, seeking further information.

"Oh, yes, and so am I," Harry offered. "I always say having young folk around you keeps you from being lonely. They rekindle memories. Remind one of times and friends".

He looks cheerful enough, thought Daisy, as Harry chuckled to himself and shuffled to a table in the far corner of the room.

*

"Did you miss me yesterday, then?" asked Harry, in a friendlier tone, a couple of days later.

"Yes. Wondered where you were, Harry."

Harry grimaced. She's too familiar by far, he thought.

"Had a bit of stomach-ache," he said by way of explanation. There was a brisker manner about him this morning.

"Got some shopping to do today, love," said Harry. "A few toys and things. A few decorations like."

Daisy looked puzzled, frowned and then all at once remembered.

"The party! Your birthday soon, isn't it?"

"That's right," said Harry. "Coffee, please, and a doughnut, miss. Can't hang around talking today, you know."

As if he ever did, thought Daisy. Still, she was glad to see him looking so bright. She almost wished she could go to his party, too.

*

For a time, the days followed their normal pattern until one Saturday when Harry shuffled into the Coffee Parlour a little more quickly than usual.

"Thirty doughnuts, please," demanded Harry excitedly.

"Thirty!" cried Daisy disbelievingly. The other girl's mouth hung open stupidly.

"For the party," he added. Daisy glanced towards the cake tray and swiftly drew her hand to her mouth.

"We've ... run out!" she stuttered, sucking feverishly on a finger.

"Oh, my goodness," spluttered Harry. "I don't

know about this. I don't know at all. Your doughnuts are the best, the biggest, the most jam, the ones they'll like the most."

"Would chocolate eclairs do?" asked the other girl.

"No, they **won't**," exploded Harry, thinking of juicy, fat doughnuts. "They want the taste of jam not cream. Oh, dear. Oh, dear. Oh, dear."

"Just a moment," interjected Daisy. "I'll ring the bakery."

She returned five minutes later, a look of relief on her face.

"They'll deliver more doughnuts this afternoon."

"This **afternoon?**" Harry's expression crumpled. "I've so much to do. So much to prepare and now ... no special tea-time treat for them."

Daisy felt suddenly inspired.

"I'll deliver!" she announced.

There was silence. Avis stared at her. Harry stared at her.

"I've got a car," she continued. "Give me the address. I'll deliver them this afternoon in time for your party."

"We'll be waiting," grinned Harry delightedly.

Or did he smirk?

He shuffled away from the Coffee Parlour wondering why people were always letting him down. Oh, yes, no doubt she'd deliver the doughnuts all right but what about now, eh? What about the doughnut that should have accompanied his coffee? He hadn't had his doughnut. It was most unsatisfactory.

*

Avis was a bit full of herself. She was in charge this afternoon. True, she had nobody to supervise but her time would come. It was good practise, even for an afternoon, in case Daisy ever decided to go for good. **She'd** run things differently. **She'd** make changes. **She** had ideas. Unlike Daisy, she thought, and smiled wickedly to herself.

The doughnuts had arrived from the bakery by two and by three Daisy had packed them neatly into white boxes and had left within the half hour.

Daisy knew where Froggett Lane was and drove slowly along the narrow, winding lane looking for number twenty-four. She pulled onto the grass verge beside the small cottage, got out of her car and knocked lightly against the peeling paint on the door. She heard sounds from within which drew closer as Harry came to the door. He smiled broadly when he saw the boxes that Daisy was carrying and asked,

"Won't you come in, my dear? Won't you join us?"

Daisy hesitated for a moment.

"Well, Harry," she began. She knew he liked her calling him that.

"I don't know. A handsome, young man like

yourself and an innocent girl like me," she teased.

He hated her calling him "Harry", a mere slip of a thing, a stranger, but he disguised his distaste.

"We are all especially pleased that you are here. We're all waiting," he declared.

"Well, alright, then," conceded Daisy. "Just for a minute," and stepped inside.

From behind an inner door, Daisy could hear crackly chattering coming from a radio. The door was not tightly shut, though, and as Harry closed the front door, so the inner door was sucked open slightly by the draught of air. Daisy could see nothing through the crack. The room was in darkness. It looked as dim and dank as the entrance hall in which she now stood. She shivered even though she wasn't cold. Harry led her by the arm.

"This way, my dear," he said, taking the boxes from her.

"Okay, Harry," she replied bleakly.

Harry pushed open the door. The radio was still playing but she couldn't see it. The room was enveloped in gloomy shadow.

"Wait a moment," said Harry. She heard a click and a faint light from a table-lamp illuminated a small table and an old-fashioned radio, beside which sat a gramophone.

"I'll just get things going and then we'll have the light on," said Harry switching off the radio.

She could hear him shuffling around the room repeating, "Here we are, one for you. Here we are, one for you." He returned to the dimly lit table and from somewhere beyond her sight found a record, placed it on the turntable and slowly wound-up the gramophone. He lowered the heavy arm and Daisy began listening to "The Teddy Bears Picnic".

Harry snapped on the lights and Daisy shrieked.

Staring at her - with an unwavering gaze - was an enormous doll sitting in a high-chair. Beside this doll was yet another doll in yet another high-chair and both stared straight at her.

And then, forming a semicircle, she saw other dolls, some sitting in small chairs, some in large chairs, some on stools, some on the floor. Big dolls, small dolls, some in fancy clothes, some in plain, their eyes turned towards the table in the centre of their midst, all staring at the food. Some held balloons, some wore coloured hats. Still more dolls were grouped behind these dolls but **all** the dolls had one thing in common. Balanced on their laps was a plate and balanced on each plate was a doughnut.

Harry was behind her. He pulled the scarf tightly around her neck.

Daisy tried screaming but neither sound nor breath would come. Tighter and tighter he pulled until her body grew limp and she sank to the floor. As she lay there, motionless, Harry forced her lips apart, opened a paper bag, took out a doughnut and placed it in her mouth.

"That'll teach her," he said to his young friends. "She made me go without my doughnut this morning."

It was Monday morning and Avis was wondering where Daisy had got to. It just wasn't like Lady Perfect to be late. She was on the point of sneaking to the manager to let him know when Harry shuffled in.

"Coffee and a doughnut please," he said politely. Avis stared at him coldly. She wouldn't be like

Daisy. None of this "Harry" stuff. She wanted no social chit-chat with this old man. Daisy hadn't turned up for work and *she* was in charge. Things were going to be different.

Harry had his mouth full of doughnut when he felt the heavy hand on his shoulder. He glanced up and seemed surprised to see three policemen standing behind him.

"Harry Coker?" one of them asked.

*

On her way home that evening, Avis counted her blessings.

"I thought they'd **come** for me," she joked to herself. She shivered in the coolness of the night and pulled her coat closer to her body. For a moment or two she had thought her manager had caught her stealing money from the till when she cashed up at night.

She suddenly felt very guilty, too, about throwing thirty doughnuts into the rubbish bin last Saturday morning just to spite Daisy. Just to catch her out.

Google: Kindle Store/Terence Braverman

amazon/books/terence braverman

terry@terrybraverman.co.uk

updates:

www.noteablemusic.co.uk

* * *

AVAILABLE BOOKS (September 2024)

'Whiskers, Wings and Bushy Tails'

(Stories from The Undermead Woods) book series for children.

Large print and double line spacing

The series includes the following titles (Sept. 2020)

The Inner Mystic Circle

The Race

Curly Cat

Dotty Dormouse

Blackberry Pie

George and the

Magic Jigsaw

Rain! Rain! Rain!

Where is Dotty Dormouse?

Tap! Tap! Tap!

SwaggerWagger

Three Wheels and a Bell

The Chase

Blackberry Bluff

Rebellion

Autumn

Quiz Night

Black as Night

Sheepish Singing Sisters

Ollie Owl's Experiment (Part Two)

Good Deeds and Evil Intentions

The New Age of Barter

The Mouse That Scored

Links of Gold

Buttercups and Daisies

The Tick-Tock 'Tective Agency and the Case of

The Missing Tiddles

The Mysterious Case of the Missing Scarecrow

Carrots

Woof! Woof! *(Percy Pigeon is behaving strangely ... once again... and Ollie Owl is determined to put his wisdom. and the academic books on the shelves of his library, to correct* matters for the citizens (the whiskered, winged, and bushy-tailed of Undermead.. Doctor Deer O'Dear has a cure ... or has he? Why is Swagger Wagger, the aristocratic Japanese Chin Dog, aggrieved? Has Percy a suitable poem to explain away his behaviour ... or is he simply playing games?

A shorter tale this time but easy-to-read style for juniors. Larger print and well-spaced lines. Coloured pictures.

The entire series is available through Amazon in both paperback and eBook form.)

These are some of the inhabitants of The Undermead Woods to be found in the series 'Whiskers, Wings and Bushy Tails'

Bad Boy Badger and the Snooty Ooty Gang

Ollie Owl

Curly Cat

Ebenezer Eagle

Rocky Ram and The Sheeptones

Dotty Dormouse

Lord Hawley

Swagger Wagger the Pekinese Chin Dog

Doctor Deer O'Dear

Tommy Tortoise and Sammy Snail

Percy Pigeon

The Cuckoo Clock

Mrs Woodmouse of The Fruit and Nut Shop

The Home for Elderly and Retired Rats and other Rodents

Dancing Mice

Ferdinand Fox

The Scarecrow, Dotty and Woolly Dormouse, Roland Rabbit, Willy Worm, Squeaky Squirrel, Spindly Spider and more.

Large print and double line spacing

GENERAL BOOKS FOR YOUNG READERS

Millie Manx (The Tale of a Tail)

Granddad Remembers (But is he telling the truth?)

Ninky and Nurdle (Stories from Noodle-Land)

The Playground of Dreams

What Can I Do When It's Raining Outside?

Buggy Babes

CRIME

Time to Kill

Stage Fright

The Potato Eaters / Revolving Doors (Fiction based on fact)

Donald Dangle is on The Point of Murder

ROMANCE

The Man from Blue Anchor

The Night of The Great Storm

A TWIST IN THE TALE

Open Pandora's Box and what will you find?

(25 stories with 'a twist in the tale')

A Night at the Castle

Baby Jane

The Little Bedroom

Bulls Eye

A Problem at School

A Running Joke

The Cure

Old Rocker

The New Appointment

The Sunflower

The Christmas Fairy

Pressure

Promotion

Knock, Knock, Knock

The Letter

Printed in Great Britain
by Amazon